Animal  Lives

GORILLAS

Sally Morgan

QED Publishing

D0258730

Copyright © QED Publishing 2005

First published in the UK in 2005 by
QED Publishing
A Quarto Group company
226 City Road
London EC1V 2TT

www.qed-publishing.com

A Catalogue record for this book is
available from the British Library.

ISBN 1 84538 405 9

Written by Sally Morgan
Designed by Q2A Solutions
Editor Tom Jackson
Map by PCGraphics (UK) Ltd

Publisher Steve Evans
Creative Director Louise Morley
Editorial Manager Jean Coppendale

Printed and bound in China

Picture Credits

Getty: Art Wolfe 4–5, John Giustina 7, Ken
Lucas 12, Stan Osolinski 13, Steve Bloom 18,
Gary Randall 26
Corbis: Front cover Martin Harvey, Kevin
Schafer 5, Staffan Widstrand 15, Kennan
Ward 17, 21, Mary Ann McDonald 23, Martin
Harvey 24, 28–29, Tom Brakefield 30
Still Pictures: Michel Gunther 6, Martin
Harvey 8–9, 11, 19, 22, Tom Murphy/WWI 14,
Kevin Schafer 20, 30, Fritz Polking 25, 30
Ecoscene: Robert Pickett 10, Fritz Polking 16,
Karl Ammann 29
FLPA/Minden Pictures: Konrad Wothe 27

The words in **bold**
are explained in the
Glossary on page 31.

Contents

The gorilla

The gorilla is the world's largest **primate**; other primates include monkeys and chimpanzees. People are also primates, and gorillas are one of our closest relatives. Gorillas are gentle, clever animals and some gorillas in captivity have even learned a few words in sign language. Gorillas and other primates are **mammals**. These are animals that have hair and give birth to live young. Other mammals include lions, seals and elephants.

Big bodies

Gorillas are hairy animals with long arms. They have a bulky body with a broad chest. The males are twice as big as the females. Older males have white hairs on their backs and are called **silverbacks**.

Many people think that gorillas are dangerous, but they rarely attack humans. Sadly, people still hunt and kill gorillas and there is only a small number of them left in the world.

A gorilla is a very strong and powerful animal.

Gorilla

The name gorilla means 'hairy person' and was first used by an explorer from North Africa 2500 years ago.

fact

Gorillas have a large head with a bulging forehead, tiny ears and small brown eyes.

5

Types of gorilla

There is only one **species**, or type, of gorilla. However, this species is divided into three **subspecies**. These are the mountain gorilla, the western lowland gorilla and the eastern lowland gorilla.

All three subspecies are about the same size. The males are about 170cm tall and weigh about 160kg.

The mountain gorilla has long hair to keep it warm in the cold mountain forests.

The differences

One way of telling the subspecies apart is by the colour of their hair. The western lowland gorilla has brown hair, while the other two types have black hair.

The western lowland gorilla's nose is also wider than those of the other subspecies.

The western lowland gorilla has reddish hair on its forehead.

Gorilla numbers	
Western lowland	110 500
Eastern lowland	10 500
Mountain gorilla	less than 600

Where do gorillas live?

Mountain gorillas live in chilly forests that are 3000m above sea level.

Wild gorillas
live in the
forests of Africa.
Once these forests
spread right across
Central Africa. However,
today many of the forests have
been cut down and the gorillas survive
in a few small areas.

   Western lowland gorillas are found mostly in the
western Congo and Gabon. Eastern lowland gorillas
live in the eastern Congo. Mountain gorillas are found
in the mountains of Rwanda, Uganda and eastern Congo.

Gorilla habitats

Gorillas live in forests, where there is a good supply of food. They are too big to move around much in very thick forest, so gorillas sit in forest clearings in family groups playing, eating and grooming.

Lowland gorillas live in forests where the climate is hot all year, although it rains almost every day. Mountain gorillas live in forests that grow on the slopes of volcanoes. Here it is often cloudy and cold.

Gorilla

About 550 gorillas are kept in zoos and wildlife parks in case the wild gorillas become extinct.

fact

North America

Atlantic Ocean

Europe

Asia

Africa

Pacific Ocean

Pacific Ocean

South America

Indian Ocean

Australia

Southern Ocean

Antarctica

Areas where gorillas are found.

Living in a group

Gorillas live in family groups of between three and 30 animals. A typical gorilla family consists of one adult male (the silverback), three or four adult females and five or six youngsters of varying ages. The most important individual is the silverback, who is head of the group.

Silverback males are so called because of the white hair that looks like a saddle on their back.

Leaving the family group

The youngsters live with their family until they reach ten years old. Then some of the female gorillas may move to join other groups.

All the younger males are driven away by the silverback by the time they are 15. There is room for only one adult male in a family. The younger males live alone for many years until they form their own group or take one over.

Gorilla

Few forest animals attack gorillas. Their worst enemies are human hunters, who shoot gorillas for their meat.

fact

The ages of family members can range from newborns to gorillas more than 30 years old.

Beginning life

Gorillas do not have a **breeding season** so babies are born at any time of the year. The female gorilla is **pregnant** for about 8½ months. She gives birth to a single baby that weighs just 2kg. Newborn babies have grey-pink skin and a thin covering of hair. The mother feeds her baby on milk for three years. After about two years, the youngster eats some solid food as well.

The female gorilla feeds her baby with milk that is rich in protein and fat.

This youngster is old enough to ride on its mother's back.

Gorilla

In the wild, under half of young gorillas die before they are three years old.

fact

Crawling and walking

At first, the mother carries her baby everywhere. At about two months, the baby starts to crawl. It begins to ride on its mother's back at four months and is walking at nine months.

Sometimes mothers give birth to twins. Only one of the babies will survive because the mother cannot carry both of them.

Growing up

While they play, young gorillas are learning to use their bodies and to communicate.

The young gorillas in a family all play together. Playtime is during the middle of the day when the older gorillas are having a rest. The adults keep watch over their young and sometimes they join in with the games. This helps the youngsters learn how to behave properly with other gorillas, especially with the big silverback.

14

Watch and learn

A young gorilla learns by watching its mother. This is how the young gorilla finds out which foods are good and safe to eat. The mother also shows the youngster how to use sticks and other tools to collect food.

A mother will teach and protect her youngster for about four years. Then she will be ready to have another baby. Female gorillas have three or four babies in their lifetime.

Gorilla

When an adult male takes over a family group, he may kill some of the baby gorillas that belonged to the previous silverback.

fact

Young gorillas spend much of the day exploring their surroundings.

15

Feeding

Gorillas are **omnivores**. This means that they eat both animals and plants. Although most of their food is leaves, they also eat fruits, roots, flowers, grass, mushrooms and small insects. A gorilla's favourite foods are bamboo, thistles and wild celery. Gorillas do not drink anything as they get all the water they need from the food that they eat.

Gorillas can grip food with their feet using their big toe like a thumb.

Gorillas stand on their hind legs to reach branches that have leaves or fruits.

Searching for food

A family group moves slowly through the forest searching for food. They feed most in the morning and afternoon.

Gorillas eat mainly leaves and roots, which make them feel full very quickly. They sit and rest in the middle of the day to help **digest** their food.

Gorilla

A full grown male gorilla eats about 23kg of food every day. That is more than seven 3kg bags of potatoes.

fact

17

Teeth

The teeth of the gorilla are good at grinding up plant food. Leaves and stems are very tough and need to be chewed a lot before they can be swallowed.

Gorillas have four types of teeth. The small front teeth are called incisors, which are used for biting. Next there are four pointed canines. These are used for fighting, not eating. Behind the canines are the premolars and molars. These are ridged teeth that are good for grinding food into a paste.

Male gorillas open their mouths to show off their dangerous canines when they are angry with another gorilla.

Milk teeth

Gorillas grow two sets of teeth just like people. A young gorilla's **milk teeth** are small and gradually fall out. They are replaced by a set of large permanent teeth that grow when the gorilla is about three years old.

Gorilla

A male gorilla's canine teeth are longer than a female's. The males use them to frighten away attackers.

fact

Gorillas have very strong jaws, which help them to chew.

Gorilla movement

Gorillas can stand on their hind legs, but they cannot walk very far like this because their bodies are too heavy. Instead they walk on all fours, using both their arms and legs. Gorillas put their weight on the knuckles of their fist, not on their palms. This is known as knuckle-walking.

Gorillas can knuckle-walk because they have long arms that reach to the ground.

Young gorillas are still light enough to climb up trees and swing in the branches

Gorilla

A male gorilla is about 15cm shorter than an average human but its arms are 30cm longer.

fact

Running and climbing

Gorillas walk most of the time, but they can run a short way if needed. When they feel in danger, gorillas charge at their attackers to scare them away. They run with their arms swinging by their sides. Youngsters also like to explore in trees. They use their long arms to pull themselves up into the branches.

Gorilla senses

Gorilla's have five senses – hearing, sight, smell, taste and touch – just like a person. A gorilla needs to use all of its senses to survive in the forest.

Finding food

Gorillas have good eyesight. They use it to find tasty food in the forest. Gorillas can see in colour so they can spot the ripest fruits. Gorillas then check the food is good to eat by smelling and tasting it.

A gorilla's eyes point forwards. This helps it to judge distances and see detail clearly.

Gorilla

Male gorillas produce a strong smell from their armpits when they are angry or frightened.

fact

22

Listening out

The trees of the forest stop gorillas seeing into the distance very easily. This means they have to rely on their hearing to find each other and to detect danger. Gorillas become very alert if they hear an unusual noise. Gorillas can see things close up very well, which helps them when they are grooming.

As well as hearing strangers, gorillas can smell them approaching.

Living space

A family of gorillas lives in an area called a **territory**, where they find all of their food. A territory can be as big as 50 square kilometres. The territory of one group often overlaps with the territories of other families. Gorillas do not move very far each day, and they rarely meet their neighbours.

The family group moves to a new feeding spot every day.

Building nests

Gorillas sleep for about 13 hours a night, and they also rest at midday. At dusk, each gorilla builds a sleeping nest by bending branches to form a cushion. The nest may be on the ground or in low branches. Youngsters share their mother's nest until they are about three years old.

A day in the life of a gorilla

6am–8am:	Wake up
8am–10am:	Eat
10am-2pm:	Eat, play, relax and sleep
2pm–5pm:	Walk through the forest, travelling anywhere between 100m and 1800m, feeding on the way
5pm–6pm:	Build nest
6pm–6am:	Sleep

A gorilla's nest is much warmer than sleeping on the cold ground.

25

Communication

Gorillas are quiet animals, but they do use sounds to talk to each other. They can make about 25 different sounds, including screams, grunts and barks. Gorillas have moods, just like people. For example, they can be angry, happy, sad and jealous. They even laugh when they are tickled.

Roars and hoots can carry thousands of metres through the forest.

Meeting strangers

When a group of gorillas meets a strange family, the females and young run away. The big males stay to defend their territories.

Gorillas try to frighten each other by standing up on their back legs to look bigger. They beat their chest, roar and wave their arms around. Sometimes they tear off branches and charge at each other. Usually one of the males runs away.

Gorilla fact

Koko is a captive gorilla who has learned sign language. She knows the signs for about 1000 words and understands 2000 words of spoken English.

Grooming each other's fur helps gorillas in a family to stay friends.

Gorillas under threat

Each year, there are fewer gorillas living in the wild. Sadly these amazing animals are in danger of becoming **extinct**.

The main threat to gorillas is from people cutting down their forest home. The forests are being cleared to make more space for farms. Some gorillas are killed by hunters who sell the meat.

Money from gorilla-watching could be used to protect more gorillas.

Saving the gorillas

The best way to save the gorillas is to protect their **habitat** and stop the hunting. The mountain gorillas are the most threatened. Many of them live in nature reserves and tourists pay to see them in the wild. The tourists' money is used to protect the gorillas and help local people. But hunters still sometimes kill the gorillas in the reserves.

This baby gorilla is an orphan. Its mother was killed and now it will be sold as a pet.

Gorilla

Each year more than 500 lowland gorillas are killed for food in the Congo.

fact

Life cycle

Most female gorillas have their first baby when they are about ten years old. Male gorillas can only breed once they have taken control of a family. Most new silverbacks are about 20 years old. Many males never breed. Gorillas live for about 35 years in the wild and as long as 50 years in zoos.

Youngster

Adolescent

Mature silverback

Glossary

breeding season time of year when animals mate and have babies

digest to break down food in the stomach into simple substances

extinct when there are no more of a species left

habitat the place in which an animal or plant lives

mammal an animal that is covered in hair and suckles, or feeds, newborns with milk

milk teeth name given to the first set of teeth a mammal has. These fall out and are replaced by larger teeth.

omnivore an animal that eats a mixed diet of plant and animal food

pregnant a female animal that has a baby developing inside her

primate a type of mammal that has hands and feet and a large brain

silverback the name given to a fully grown male that leads a family group

species a group of animals that look alike and can produce young

subspecies groups within a species that look slightly different from each other

territory an area where a gorilla finds all its food

Index